Absolute Crime Presents:

The Fruitvale Station Shooting

ABSO|UTE CR|ME

By Fergus Mason

Absolute Crime Books

www.absolutecrime.com

Table of Contents

About Us

Absolute Crime publishes only the best true crime literature. Our focus is on the crimes that you've probably never heard of, but you are fascinated to read more about. With each engaging and gripping story, we try to let readers relive moments in history that some people have tried to forget.

Remember, our books are not meant for the faint at heart. We don't hold back—if a crime is bloody, we let the words splatter across the page so you can experience the crime in the most horrifying way!

If you enjoy this book, please visit our homepage to see other books we offer; if you have any feedback, we'd love to hear from you!

Prologue

Fruitvale BART Station, Oakland, Alameda County, CA - 2:00 a.m., Jan 1, 2009

The BART police were nervous. San Francisco Bay is a lively area with a busy social life, but usually it's pretty good-natured. The Bay's counterculture reputation has softened over the years and it's become more of a fun, quirky place than a center of rebellion against society. There is social deprivation though - inevitable in a conurbation that houses over 7 million people from every ethnic group you could imagine - and sometimes fun can spill over into violence.

Of course violence is always more likely when alcohol is involved, and with the New Year celebrations just starting to wind down there was plenty of it around now. That was bad enough. Add guns to the mix and it could get really ugly, and that's why the police were nervous. There had been two firearms incidents in the last hour. A fight had broken out at Embarcadero Station, and although details weren't clear yet a revolver had been recovered. Then, just down the line at West Oakland, a teenage boy with a loaded semi-automatic had jumped off the platform while running from police and was in the hospital with multiple fractures.

Dennis Zafiratos was nervous, too. He'd been celebrating at Embarcadero and now he was riding the BART Dublin/Pleasanton line home to Castro Valley. BART is usually a safe enough way to travel, but a bad atmosphere had developed on the trip out of the city. Now, as the train pulled into West Oakland, words had turned to punches. Two men, one white and one black, were swinging away at each other. Their friends, black on one side and mostly Latino on the other, were pushing each other and exchanging insults. Zafiratos stayed out of it; he just wanted to get home. He had another seven stations to go, though, and he hoped these assholes weren't going to keep it up the whole way.

The train stopped and a dozen passengers quickly disembarked, some of them throwing nervous or angry glances behind. Then the doors closed and the train pulled out. The next stop was Lake Merritt, where pretty much the same scene was repeated. After that came Fruitvale. More passengers spilled out, some of them looking like they just wanted to get away from the scene inside the car. A couple of the fighters stumbled out, too. Then Zafiratos saw a BART policeman run out onto the platform.

Former Marine Tony Pirone and his partner Marysol Domenici were on the lower floor of the station booking a drunk when a message came through on his radio. There were reports of fighting on board a train coming out from Embarcadero through West Oakland. They'd put out a call for support and reinforcements were on the way, including two officers who'd been dealing with witnesses at West Oakland, but the train was likely to get there first. Could they deal with it? Pirone said he could. Leaving Domenici to deal with the inebriated partygoer he headed upstairs to find the train already at the platform.

Pirone found the platform nearly empty; most of the disembarking passengers had already headed downstairs. The train was waiting at the platform with the car doors open. He drew his Taser electroshock gun and walked to the front car. Fingers started pointing at young men, and Pirone ordered them out of the car one by one. "You, get the f**k out," he yelled. "Out the car." A couple obeyed, and were pushed towards the back wall of the platform. Others ignored him; they were roughly seized and dragged out by the burly six foot, one inch officer.

With five suspects on the platform Pirone decided he needed help, and radioed Domenici to call her upstairs. She arrived in moments and looked around, then drew her own Taser. This wasn't a scene she liked very much; Pirone was trying to control five young men by himself, and many of the passengers on the train seemed angry. As Pirone forced one of the men to the platform she started talking to three others who were standing against the wall. They argued with her, protesting their innocence.

Pirone disagreed. Leaving the other man on the ground he walked over beside Domenici. One of the three, 22-year-old Oscar Grant III, opened his mouth to say something. Pirone never gave him a chance; he punched Grant straight in the face, bouncing him off the wall and leaving him staggering. With his other hand he raised the Taser and shouted at the other two, "Get down on the floor. Go on, sit down." Under the threat of the electric gun they did. Pirone swore at Grant and looked round at the developing situation.

Now more BART officers clattered out onto the platform. Among them Pirone recognized the veteran Jon Woffinden and his partner Johannes Mehserle. Only two years on the force but bigger even than Pirone, Mehserle was an intimidating presence. As Woffinden turned to deal with half a dozen young men who seemed to want to get to the group against the wall, Pirone pointed at Mehserle and said, "Watch them. Don't let them get away." Mehserle now drew his own Taser and covered the three with it. Panicking at having so many of the weapons aimed at him Grant yelled, "Don't Taser me, I have a four year old daughter." Then Pirone changed his mind again.

"I want him arrested," he said, pointing at Grant, "Get the cuffs on him." Mehserle holstered his Taser and moved forward. He and another cop took hold of Grant and forced him to his knees, then flat on his stomach. Pirone joined in, kneeling on Grant's back to pin him down as Mehserle struggled to get his arms round.

Grant knew the drill; he'd been cuffed before. This time he was struggling to get air, though. He'd been pushed down across the legs of his friend Carlos Reyes and Pirone's 210 pound weight was crushing the wind out of him. He struggled to push himself up slightly and get some space. When one of the cops holding him suddenly stood up he thought he was being allowed to breathe properly. He was wrong.

Mehserle took a step back and shouted "Tony, stand back! I'm going to Tase him." He drew, brought his hand up and squeezed the trigger. Not the trigger of his Taser, though. The whole station seemed to freeze as the shot crashed out.

Chapter 1: Oscar Grant

Oscar Juliuss Grant III was born on February 27, 1986 to Oscar Grant Jr. and Wanda Johnson. His birthplace was Highland Hospital in Oakland; his mother lived in Hayward. By the time Grant was born Johnson was a single parent. Oscar Grant Jr. was in the state prison at Vacaville serving life for murder, where he remains today.[i] The devoutly religious Johnson took on the challenge of raising her son alone, with only occasional visits to his father. She was lucky; unlike many other single parents in low-income areas she could count on support from an extended family, so Grant was often looked after by uncles and grandparents. Johnson also held down a steady job at UPS. Eventually advancing to a supervisory position, she had no illusions about the importance of work and tried to pass this attitude on to her children.

As a boy, Grant loved fishing and playing baseball and basketball. He was also active in his local congregation, Palma Ceia Baptist Church, where he would pray enthusiastically in front of the assembly. He went to San Lorenzo High School and then Mount Eden High until dropping out in 10th grade.[ii] He was an outgoing and a bright student, but he'd made some bad choices in his friends and that got him into trouble. He was also affected by his home life; the absence of his father upset him, and he envied friends who had both parents around.

After school Grant started getting into increasing trouble with the law. He was arrested five times, at first for small offences like driving with broken lights. Then he spent time in jail for drug dealing after Hayward police caught him selling Ecstasy; in his statement he said he was earning $1,000 to $1,500 a week from dealing. He had a stable family life, though. He and long-term girlfriend Sofina Mesa had a daughter in 2005 and Grant doted on her. He also worked on and off. His older sister was a manager with Kentucky Fried Chicken and had run restaurants in the East Bay, and she gave Oscar chances whenever she could, so he managed to get jobs at several branches.

In October 2006 Grant was involved in a traffic stop carried out by San Leandro police. He had a loaded .380 pistol on him and decided to flee.[iii] He made for his home in Hayward, but before he got there police cornered him near a gas station. Grant threw his gun away and bolted into the station. Police followed him in and there was a struggle. When Grant wouldn't come quietly one of the officers, who was carrying a Taser, used it on him. He was arrested and charged with possession of an illegal firearm, and ended up sentenced to 16 months in prison. He was also left with a fear of being Tased again. Describing the experience, he told Mesa that he wouldn't wish a Taser discharge on anyone.[iv] Grant spent his sentence in Alameda County Jail and Santa Rita Jail in Dublin, until his release in September 2008. At New Year he was still on parole.

Grant might have ended up in prison on a serious charge, but the signs are that he was making an effort this time. While in Santa Rita he earned his GED and gained extra privileges for good behavior. He also developed a new interest; cutting hair. Practicing on his fellow inmates made him think of becoming a barber, an ambition he confided to his mother on Christmas Day just a week before he was shot. Wanda Johnson says her son opened up to her about his mistakes that day during a family gathering at her mother's home; he realized that he'd made mistakes and wanted to settle down. While he planned how to get a start at barbering he found a job at Farmer Joe's, an Oakland organic market, as a butcher. His grandmother Bonnie Johnson says he enjoyed helping customers; once he called her to say a customer wanted help cooking a piece of fish, and asked her for her secret recipe.

The various accounts of Oscar Grant paint a complex picture. A troubled young man who'd had more than his fair share of trouble with the law - and it's no use pretending he was an innocent victim in all of this - he finally seemed to be making a real effort to turn his life around. He'd dropped out of school, like many of his peers, but had taken the chance to get his GED in prison. Peer pressure and a jailed father have a powerful ability to steer someone in the wrong direction but from what his mother said - and she's a remarkable, credible figure - he had realized where he was going wrong. Many young inner city men are serial fathers, but Grant was different; he was genuinely devoted to his girlfriend and young daughter, and wanted to give them the best he could afford. Even before his last prison sentence he'd at least made some effort to find work and he seemed enthusiastic about his new job at Farmer Joe's. He'd not exactly made the most of his life so far but, with the support of a strong family, he had the potential to start again. He seems to have realized that in the weeks before his death.

Chapter 2: Johannes Mehserle

Johannes Sebastian Mehserle's background couldn't have been more different from Grant's. He was born in Germany in 1982 but the family moved to the Bay Area when he was four years old. Mehserle attended the newly opened New Technology High School in Napa from 1996 to his graduation in 2000. New Tech is a small school with less than 400 students, and it uses radical teaching methods; multi-disciplinary classes combine two or more traditional subjects, and it was one of the first schools to supply a computer for every student. The emphasis is on problem solving and technology and graduation rates are extremely high; 98% of students graduate, and 95% go on to post secondary education against an average of under 40% in other Napa Valley high schools. Mehserle was one of the 95%. After high school he went on to college in Napa and Monterey, and finally to Sonoma State University. He majored in business, but a friend in the police got him interested in law enforcement. Returning to Napa Valley College he went through their police academy; in 2006 he graduated from the program with high marks, one of the top five in his class academically and with good marks in physical subjects too. In March 2007 he was accepted by the BART Police.

By New Year's Day 2009 Mehserle was an accepted member of the force. Still partnered with a more experienced officer who could act as a mentor, nevertheless he'd settled into the job and seen a lot of what police get confronted with. He'd even faced up to armed robbers just weeks before.

Mehserle had a pretty good reputation among his coworkers. Colleagues didn't think of him as an aggressive officer, and nobody had put in a serious complaint about him. Of course as a police officer it's inevitable that complaints will be made, but a lot of them are frivolous. Nothing had been said about Mehserle that caused his bosses any concern. The only real allegation against him surfaced after he was arrested for shooting Oscar Grant; Kenneth Carrethers, a 41-year-old with a record for theft and housebreaking, claimed Mehserle had beaten him in November 2008 after he tried to walk away from police who were talking to him. Mehserle's report says he overheard Carrethers make insulting comments about the police, and Carrethers admits this. There's a disagreement about what happened next though. Carrethers says he walked away and Mehserle grabbed him from behind, knocked him down and beat him. Mehserle says Carrethers became abusive and threatening and had to be restrained.[v] The problem is that Carrethers didn't complain to anyone when the incident happened and only seemed to remember that he'd been beaten up after Mehserle was arrested. He also didn't have any witnesses to back up his version of the story.

There's nothing in Mehserle's police record or earlier life that gives any clue to why he shot Oscar Grant. He wasn't aggressive or excessively violent, as his detractors suggested. He didn't seem likely to panic under stress as his defenders said, either. Whatever made him draw his pistol that night, it can't be found in his biography.

Chapter 3: New Year's Day

San Franciscans like to party, and the city is a magnet for Bay Area residents on major occasions. Every New Year one of the major attractions is a free firework display launched from boats in the Bay, and tens of thousands of people gather in the Embarcadero area to enjoy it. It's billed by the city as an alcohol-free event, but that's more a wish than an accurate description. Plenty of people will sneak in a hip flask or even a stash of beer; plenty more will head down there straight from a bar. It's guaranteed that a large percentage of the crowd will already be pretty well lit before the first rocket goes up. For many that adds to the party atmosphere, but for others it's a catalyst for trouble.

Oscar Grant, with thousands of others, had made the trip into San Francisco for the fireworks. His daughter Tatiana hadn't wanted him to go, seeming upset about being left behind, but Grant had managed to calm her down with a promise of taking her and one of her cousins to Chuck E. Cheese next day.[vi] About 10:30 p.m. he and his girlfriend Sofina left his Hayward home and headed for the city. Taking his mother's advice he rode on BART instead of driving, and his friends did the same. Now he was enjoying the show from Pier 39.

Around 1:00 a.m. a fight broke out among the crowds at the Embarcadero BART station. BART police broke it up, but as they dealt with the participants a revolver was found. California has extremely restrictive gun laws and carrying a handgun in public is a serious offence; it's a worrying event when one is recovered in a situation like this.

Shortly afterwards there was another firearms incident, this time outside the city. A teenage boy fled from police at West Oakland BART station, and he was brandishing a semiautomatic pistol. He didn't fire it, but when the police recovered it later they found it was loaded. This incident ended badly as the boy jumped down onto the tracks in an attempt to evade arrest; he suffered several fractures and wound up in hospital. Two BART officers who attended the incident then collected statements from witnesses. They were Johannes Mehserle and his partner Jon Woffinden, an eleven-year police veteran who'd been with the BART force for two years after spending eight years at Pleasant Hill and 18 months at Moraga.

Both these incidents had happened on the BART system, and West Oakland is only two stops down the line from Fruitvale. Police officers get nervous at the thought of guns and crowds; there's just too much potential for things to get out of control. Even a trained shot can't guarantee all their rounds will be on target under the stress of a real shooting incident, and a criminal with a gun is likely to spray shots everywhere. If someone started shooting a lot of people could get hurt. The reports of weapons also put the thought at the front of everyone's minds; if another violent incident happened now the police would all have the thought in their heads that a pistol could be drawn, and they'd be ready to go for their own weapons at the first hint of a threat.

When the engineer on a train pulling out of West Oakland reported trouble on board there was no mention of guns, but what he did say was nearly as bad. Two groups of young men had got themselves into a dispute and it had escalated to thrown punches. With the boiling point lowered by alcohol it must have been a frightening experience for the other passengers on the packed train, and the BART police would have seen it as potentially serious.

Two BART officers were already at Fruitvale Station. Tony Pirone had been on the BART force for five years; before that he'd been in the United States Marine Corps, then done a stint with the police at Lawrence Livermore laboratory.[vii] Perhaps he hadn't quite shaken off the ethos of the Marine Corps, because he had a reputation for being hard-nosed and aggressive.[viii] With him was Marysol Domenici. Just after 2:00 a.m. they were downstairs in the station's entry hall talking to a drunk.

When the call came in about the fight on the train Pirone left Domenici to deal with the drunk and ran upstairs to the southbound platform. The train had already arrived and was now waiting at the platform. Pirone drew his Taser and approached the lead car of the train, where the fight had been reported. Now an element of confusion began to creep into the picture. The fight was between racially mixed groups, and accounts from the train suggest that a white man, 34 year old David Horowitch, had Grant in a headlock and was punching him. According to other passengers someone in Grant's group had insulted Horowitch's son, provoking the fight, but Horowitch himself later denied fighting and said he had "no problem" with Grant. Of course Horowitch had reason to deny fighting even if he had been; he was on parole after a term for drug dealing in Alameda County Jail, where he'd got to know Grant, and fighting in public would have violated the parole terms and put him back inside. The sparring groups also contained several Latinos. Somewhere along the chain from the passengers to the train driver and finally the police, though, information got lost; the call that Pirone received said the trouble was coming from a group of black males. Now Horowitch slipped away towards the third car as Pirone started looking for the troublemakers.

Pirone was up to the train now. From platform video footage it almost looks like he'd fallen back on his Marine training, dominating the situation with a threat of force. Taser in hand, he approached the door of the lead car and started questioning passengers. Soon fingers started pointing at those who'd been involved in the fight, and Pirone began hauling them out onto the platform. Big and aggressive, he had no problems at first; one by one young men were dragged from the car and pushed towards the wall at the back of the platform. In all he singled out five men from the group and got them lined up against the wall as support started to arrive. Witnesses say he used some force to do this; Michael Greer, a friend of Grant's, was grabbed from behind with an armlock around his neck, and others described being physically pulled off the train and thrown against the wall.[ix]

Passenger Pamela Caneva was struck by how aggressive Pirone was.

Sofina Mesa had already left the train. Instead of returning home with Grant she planned to spend the night with a friend who lived near Fruitvale station, and she'd headed downstairs with two other girls before the confrontation began. Now she heard a commotion begin above her, and saw police running into the station and heading for the platform. She reached in her bag for her cell phone.

Within minutes there were seven BART officers in the station or heading there, and managing the situation should have been easy. Other passengers had issues with what was going on, though, and what should have been simple started to get complicated. Groups of passengers were challenging the police and filming the developing incident on their phones, and tempers started to flare all round.

Chapter 4: The Platform

When Mehserle reached Fruitvale Station, he said later, he heard the uproar from the platform as soon as he got out of the car.[x] He and Woffinden ran up the stairs to the southbound platform and found a scene of chaos. Pirone had picked out his suspects, but now he was finding it difficult to control them as the crowd started to get involved. Initially he'd pushed all five against the wall and he was using his Taser to intimidate them. They weren't happy, though, and many in the crowd were loudly supporting them. Pirone called for Domenici to join him upstairs, which she did, but the trouble continued.

Grant and his friends were protesting being detained, and Pirone was running out of patience. Domenici had three of them - including Grant - against the wall and was arguing with them, and Pirone decided to assert his authority. Walking over to the group, he punched Grant in the face, sending him reeling. As the young man put his hands up to ward off further blows Pirone pointed his Taser at the other two and ordered them to sit down; they did.

Mehserle and Woffinden came out on the platform and raced forward to join their colleagues. Woffinden was quickly distracted by members of the crowd trying to push their way forward to the center of the action, and with over 300 people in the train and on the platform he was soon having a hard time. Mehserle managed to get to the wall, where Pirone was working out what to do next. He had his Taser drawn and was pointing it at the detainees. Grant, who dreaded getting another shock, pleaded, "Don't Taser me! I have a four year old daughter."

Grant's phone started ringing in his pocket. Now sitting against the wall and still stunned from Pirone's punch, he couldn't answer it. A minute later it started to ring again, though, and he managed to get it out. Looking at the number he saw it was Mesa calling. He answered and managed to say, quickly, "They are beating us up for no reason. I'll call you back."[xi] The call was cut off before she could respond.

Shortly after Mehserle and Woffinden reached the platform some sort of dispute broke out between Pirone and Grant. Cell phone footage showed Pirone calling Grant a "Bitch-ass nigger." Pirone maintains that Grant used the phrase on him and he was repeating it back.[xii] Other witnesses deny that - and Grant can't be heard shouting it on any of the recordings - and it has been questioned why Grant would use the insult on Pirone, who is white. Pirone now ordered Mehserle and another officer to put Grant on the ground and cuff him. The two of them grabbed him and got him down on the platform. Pirone knelt on his back, pinning him down - and across Carlos Reyes' legs. Now Mehserle began trying to haul Grant's hands behind his back to get the cuffs on, but he immediately ran into problems. Grant was struggling on the ground, possibly in an attempt to avoid the cuffs but more likely because being forced onto Reyes' legs by the considerable weight of Pirone was painful. Reyes himself was now calling for the officers to get Grant off his legs.[xiii] It was chaos, and the noise level just kept rising. A small group was trying to push their way in to help Grant and the others, and an increasingly frightened Woffinden was holding them off.[xiv] Shouts were coming in from all directions and stress levels were rising.

It was 2:11 am. Downstairs Mesa tried to call Grant again, but he didn't pick up. Then she heard a loud pop from the direction of the platform. She looked at her friends. "Someone's been shot," she said.

Chapter 5: The Weapons

Johannes Mehserle's defense would come to rest on the fact that he was carrying two weapons that night, both of which were roughly the same size and operated in a fairly similar manner but with very different effects. One of these was his service pistol; the other was an electroshock weapon designed to incapacitate violent individuals without causing permanent harm.

The Pistol

The standard sidearm of the BART Police is the SIG Sauer P226 semiautomatic pistol. Schweizerische Industrie Gesellschaft is a Swiss firearms company, which to get around the strict Swiss laws on exporting weapons entered into a partnership with German gun manufacturer J.P. Sauer und Sohn; SIG would design weapons and Sauer would produce them in Germany. Sauer later bought out SIG.

The first product of the partnership was the SIG P220 pistol, a high quality design chambered for 9mm Parabellum that accepted an 8-round magazine. In 1984 a high capacity version taking a 15-round magazine, the P226, was entered in the US Army's service pistol trials. It was beaten on cost grounds by the Beretta 92F, but most experts rate the P226 as a far superior weapon. Although rejected by the US military (at first - the compact P228 version is now issued as the M11) it was adopted by the British SAS and several other militaries, then became popular with US police departments and federal law enforcement agencies. As the US market is slightly prejudiced against the 9mm caliber a range of other calibers were made available including .357" SIG and .40" Smith and Wesson. The San Francisco Police Department and BART Police chose the .40 version with a 12-round magazine. The .40 cartridge isn't much liked outside the USA because it reduces magazine capacity compared to the 9mm and doesn't really offer any advantages to compensate (it's worth noting that the US Navy SEALs use the 9mm version). It's popular among US law enforcement agencies, though, and is an effective enough round for non-combat use.

The P226 is a conventional-looking automatic pistol, which appears extremely well made and in fact is much better even than that. It is double action and is fitted with a decocking lever, which allows the hammer to be safely dropped on a loaded chamber. A heavy pull on the trigger will then fire it. Because it's safe to carry with the hammer down it doesn't have a safety catch. It's a very reliable and effective pistol, just under eight inches long and weighing 34 ounces. The standard version has an alloy frame with plastic grips and a steel slide, and the entire weapon has a black finish. An accessory rail under the frame allows accessories like streamlights or laser sight modules to be fitted in front of the trigger guard, but BART Police didn't issue any of these.

Johannes Mehserle carried a P226 on every duty shift. BART police policy is to holster the service pistol on the officer's dominant side for draw with the dominant hand. In Mehserle's case it was on the right side of his belt. Officers keep their pistol in a "Level III" retention holster with a two-stage locking device, which allows a quick draw by the officer while making it extremely difficult for anyone else to snatch the weapon. Mehserle was familiar with the pistol and how it was carried; he practiced with it regularly, making an estimated 50 practice draws a week,[xv] to the point where all the actions could be carried out without thinking about them, and he could draw and use the weapon quickly and almost automatically.[xvi]

The Electroshock Weapon

Taser International was set up in 1991 to develop less lethal weapons based on electric shocks, with the intended market being self-defense. The company's name is an acronym of Thomas A. Swift's Electric Rifle, taken from the 1911 children's adventure novel *Tom Swift and His Electric Rifle*. They developed a range of weapons that use compressed air cartridges to fire two darts trailing thin wires; on impact the darts transmit an electric charge from a battery mounted in the weapon, delivering a shock to the target. Unlike earlier electric "stun guns," which worked by causing pain, the Taser weapons cause muscle incapacitation. In 1998 Taser began marketing to police departments and the X26 model, designed specifically for law enforcement use, was released in 2003.

The Taser X26 is a hand-held plastic weapon roughly the size of a large handgun, but it looks very different. The body of the weapon is directly in front of the trigger guard, not above it like in a conventional pistol, and it ends in a holder for a boxy-looking cartridge. A flashlight and laser sight are built into the body under the cartridge and a battery pack, like a smaller version of the one used on a cordless drill, snaps into the pistol grip. An ambidextrous safety catch behind the trigger can be worked with a thumb; releasing it activates the laser sight, projecting a red dot onto the point where the darts will hit, and when the trigger is pulled the darts are launched up to 35 feet away and a shower of confetti marked with the cartridge's serial number is scattered around. On impact the trailing wires transmit 50,000 volts to the darts for five seconds, and this shock over-rides the victim's nervous system; within a couple of seconds of impact they collapse. The X26 then needs to be reloaded with a new cartridge, but two electrodes on the front mean it can be pushed directly against someone's body and used as an old-style - painful - stun gun. The X26 is available in either black or yellow plastic. It's 7.55 inches long - less than a quarter inch shorter than the P226 - but only weights 10 ounces with a cartridge and battery fitted.

In 2009 BART had 60 Tasers available[xvii] but 196 sworn officers. Every officer on the force had been given six hours of training as recommended by Taser International, but they didn't have a weapon individually issued. If they could get their hands on one at the start of a shift they could carry it; otherwise they were out of luck. When the Tasers were bought in December 2008 the department followed Federal law and said they could be worn in three positions: they could be drawn with the non-dominant hand from a holster on either side of the body, or with the dominant hand from a holster on the non-dominant side. The holsters could be adjusted to allow any of those positions.

The problem was that changing a holster from one side to the other meant removing five screws and needed two tools, a screwdriver and a hex key. BART Police bought one holster for each X26, not one for each officer, and at the start of a shift officers who managed to snag a Taser would usually just wear the holster the way it was already set up. When Johannes Mehserle went on duty the night of December 31 he called colleague Emory Knudtson to borrow a yellow Taser from him;[xviii] when he got it he snapped the holster to the left side of his belt, angled so the weapon could be drawn cross-body with his right hand. BART Police regulations said this was fine, so he was carrying the weapon legally. The problem was that he'd been trained to use it for less than a month had carried it only a handful of times.[xix] On December 15 he'd been wearing one set up for a left-handed draw[xx] when he confronted two armed robbers; he'd drawn the Taser but not fired it. Now he was in the middle of a tense, chaotic situation with an unfamiliar holster setup.

Chapter 6: The Shot

Pirone had isolated five men he believed were responsible for the fight and got them up against the back wall of the platform. Now Domenici had joined him from downstairs and, maybe taking a lead from Pirone, had her Taser out too; moments later Woffinden and Mehserle ran onto the platform. With four officers and five detainees it should have been possible to control the situation without too much difficulty, but it was all going downhill quickly. Angered by Pirone's rough handling of the suspects, passengers were shouting from the train and spilling out onto the platform. Now officers were being distracted by groups of passengers arguing with them, taking attention away from what they were supposed to be doing. Pirone was getting frustrated at the delays in cuffing Grant and was trying to speed the process along, but his intervention wasn't helping.

With Grant wriggling on the ground, Reyes trapped underneath him, Mehserle trying to get the cuffs on and Pirone kneeling on top, it must have been difficult for anyone to keep track of exactly what was happening. Anyway, finally Mehserle had had enough. It's impossible to tell what was going through his head at the time. Grant's hands were now behind his back, and while he was moving multiple videos don't show the kick to the groin that Pirone claims he received at this point. Mehserle was a big man, over six feet four inches and weighing 250 pounds,[xxi] and in good shape; he should easily have been able to restrain the much smaller Grant. Maybe the crush of bodies in a small space made it awkward or maybe, keyed up by the earlier firearms incident at West Oakland, he interpreted a movement as Grant going for a weapon. Maybe his temper just snapped. Whatever was going through his head right then - and only he knows - he now made a fateful decision.

Releasing his hold on Grant, Mehserle stood up and took a step backwards. Several people heard him call, "Get back, I'm going to Tase him."[xxii] He dropped a hand to his belt - but not to the left hip, where the Taser was mounted in its cross-draw holster; he went for the *right* hip, and the holster containing the SIG pistol.

Statements from some witnesses indicate that Mehserle had trouble getting the gun out of its holster, and some of the video footage shows him making hand movements that could be consistent with trying to release the locking strap on a Taser holster (his pistol holster had a locking button, not a strap). One video also seems to show him sweeping his thumb down the side of the weapon's slide in the position where the Taser has a safety catch but the P226 doesn't. These support the claim that he drew the wrong weapon in the stress of the moment. On the other hand he didn't apparently notice that instead of a bright yellow weapon weighing just over half a pound he was now holding a black metal one more than three times the weight. Now he took aim at Grant's back and squeezed the trigger. Whether it was weapons confusion, a panicked stress reaction or deliberate malice, Mehserle fired a single shot into Grant's body from a range of barely four feet.

Leaving the muzzle at around 1,200 feet per second, a typical .40" bullet weights nearly half an ounce and has an energy of up to 500 foot pounds. Police departments usually use hollow point bullets, partly because they're more likely to incapacitate someone quickly and partly because they tend not to penetrate right through the target and endanger anyone behind them. Gunshot wounds are unpredictable, though. In this case the bullet struck Grant just to the left of his lower spine, went right through his body, hit the tile of the platform and bounced back up into his chest. Despite being damaged and destabilized by its impact with the platform it tore a wound in his right lung, causing major internal bleeding, and finished up close to his right collarbone. In a fraction of a second it had passed through most of his upper body, leaving a trail of mangled flesh over 18 inches long.

The wound was an extremely serious one; penetration of a lung often leads to a tension pneumothorax, or collapsed lung - what's also known as a sucking chest wound. What happens is the wound forms a one-way valve that allows air to be drawn into the chest cavity with each breath, but won't let it out again. A pocket of air builds up around the damaged lung and stops it inflating; the lung can't overcome the pressure of the air around it, so the victim can't draw breath fully. It can quickly worsen and interfere with the other lung, usually killing the victim through asphyxiation. Because the bullet had stopped inside Grant's body it had dumped all its energy, maximizing the damage done and increasing the rate his condition would deteriorate. While most police officers have basic first aid training very few can even begin to deal with a medical emergency like that.

Witnesses describe general confusion when the gun went off. None of the other officers had been expecting a shot; they jumped in surprise. Oscar Grant looked at Mehserle in disbelief and said, "You shot me. You shot me!"[xxiii] Mehserle seemed astonished, too. "Oh f**k," he said, "Oh, God, I shot him." Most police officers are taught that when they use a handgun they should either fire two rapid aimed shots - a "double tap" - or successive shots until the target stops moving. After firing they should keep the weapon aimed while they evaluate the situation. Mehserle didn't; he immediately holstered the pistol then clapped a hand to his face. There wasn't time to waste, though; now there was a wounded man on the platform and action was required.

Quickly recovering his composure, Mehserle knelt beside his victim and went into the routine he'd been taught. Whatever he'd been doing before Grant was not resisting now; he wasn't in any fit state to. Nevertheless Mehserle followed standard procedure and cuffed his hands behind his back. Next he located the bullet wound and pressed a hand firmly down on it. Applying direct pressure is the quickest way to stop the loss of blood, and it's often enough to keep a casualty alive until medical assistance can get there. In Grant's case it was hopeless though. Mehserle could stop the bleeding from the entry wound in Grant's back, but that wasn't the problem. Under his body, where none of the police could see, was the exit wound then the second entry wound it had made as it came back up off the platform and into Grant's chest. Combined with the internal bleeding, that added up to a lot more blood loss than Mehserle's pressure was preventing.

Within seconds of the shot another officer had radioed the dispatcher to say medical assistance was needed for a gunshot wound, although surprisingly they didn't say it was an officer-involved shooting. An ambulance was immediately sent. Reyes stayed with Grant as they waited for it, talking to him and trying to keep him conscious. Already the evidence of the lung wound was showing, as blood started to run from his mouth.

Meanwhile other officers were reacting to the shooting. They tried to collect cell phones from those who'd been filming the incident. They also had the train sent off. This decision was later criticized, because there were hundreds of potential witnesses on board and BART police had now lost track of them.

When the ambulance arrived Grant was taken to Highland Hospital in Oakland.[xxiv] The bullet had done too much damage, though. By the time he reached the hospital Grant was unconscious and his blood pressure was plummeting - both signs that can mean a pneumothorax. Blood was escaping from the wounds and his mouth, but much more was collecting in the wreckage of his chest. Although the chief of surgery and several other doctors fought to save him the bleeding couldn't be stabilized and Oscar Grant kept sinking. He was pronounced dead at around 9:00 a.m.

Chapter 7: The Aftermath

Because so many people had caught the shooting on video there was no hope of keeping the details quiet. Within hours the footage was all over the internet, and it didn't look good. There were widespread calls for action to be taken, but BART got off to a slow start. Mehserle was placed on paid leave. BART then decided to hold an internal investigation, but Mehserle short-circuited that plan. First he refused to talk to investigators. Then he pulled a surprise that put him out of reach of internal procedures - he quit.

On Wednesday, January 7, BART publicly announced that Mehserle had resigned from the force, in a move most people saw as an attempt to avoid talking to an internal inquiry.[xxv] The public wasn't happy and hundreds of people decided to demonstrate. For the most part they wanted to show their dissatisfaction at BART's response on top of their anger at the shooting itself. A rally began at the Fruitvale station around 3:00 p.m., and by 5:00 there were over a thousand people there. At this stage it was a peaceful protest; speakers addressed the growing crowd and discussed ways to campaign against police brutality. About 7:00 a march began, and the bulk of the rally moved up International Boulevard towards the downtown area.

At this point some in the crowd decided to grab the chance to cause some mayhem. As the march passed Lake Merritt station a dumpster was set on fire and a police car attacked. Riot police arrived and fired tear gas cartridges, and the violence escalated. Groups of rioters blocked intersections and started vandalizing parked cars, and the police used baton charges to push them back towards Lake Merritt. More cars were smashed up on the way, before the crowd finally began to disperse.

Oakland's mayor, Ron Dellums, arrived at about 9:00 and began to inspect the damage. As he walked towards City Hall he was questioned and confronted by locals and a crowd began to grow again, following him into Frank Ogawa Plaza. Dellums spoke from the steps of City Hall to a crowd of about 200 people. He told them that the shooting was a homicide and he had ordered an investigation, but that wasn't good enough for some. As Dellums went into City Hall some shouted "Round 2!" and groups ran into San Pablo Avenue; the destruction and arson began again. By the time police regained control around 11 they had arrested 105 people. More than 300 local businesses had been vandalized by mobs and the streets were sparkling with broken glass. As well as major companies like Sears, victims included the newly restored Fox Theater, which was due to reopen after an 11-year refurbishment, and many small businesses run by ethnic minorities. Diners in a restaurant were terrorized as rioters threw concrete through the front and tried to climb in the shattered windows. Many shopkeepers expressed support for an investigation but fury at the rioters. Leemu Topka, owner of Creative African Braids, had her store windows smashed; she said that there was no reason for protesters to break into a black-owned store and called them "stupid." Thuyen Tran said he was on the protesters' side but condemned the vandalism against his shop. Many other innocent victims couldn't see why their businesses had been attacked, either.[xxvi] The final bill for the day's damage, paid out of Oakland residents' taxes, passed $200,000.

Oscar Grant's family wanted no part of chaos like this, and on January 8 they held a press conference to condemn the violence and appeal for calm. Not everyone listened; later that day police had to disperse about 100 rioters as they threw trashcans into the streets and attacked passing cars. Violence broke out again on January 14, with more windows broken and more arrests. As hearings into Mehserle's case began they were marked by more unrest. The cause of justice for Grant now seemed to be getting hijacked by outside agitators. Local media was stating that many of the protesters weren't even from Oakland, with one commenter referring to "knuckleheads" and "wannabe Black Panthers" and warning that the continued violence played into the hands of Mehserle's defense by making it clear he couldn't get a fair trial in Oakland.[xxvii]

Also on January 7, Grant's family filed a claim for $25 million against BART.[xxviii] The attorney handling the claim, John Burris, submitted it on behalf of Grant's mother and daughter and it made clear that if BART denied the claim or failed to respond within 45 days he would sue the transit agency. In January 2010 BART settled with Sofina Mesa on behalf of Grant's daughter, setting up a $1.5 million fund that will give her payments until she's 30. Wanda Johnson did not settle.

Meanwhile Mehserle had left the state and gone to stay with a friend in Douglas County, Nevada, apparently out of fear for his own safety.[xxix] Late on January 13 he was arrested at his friend's home near Lake Tahoe and the Alameda County District Attorney announced that as the evidence indicated an intentional and unlawful killing he would be charged with murder. Extradited back to California, he was taken to the Santa Rita jail in Dublin and held in "protective custody" as prosecutors began to assemble evidence for a trial.[xxx] Alameda County DA Tom Orloff said that Mehserle's behavior was making it difficult to work out what was going on in his head at the time of the incident, because a statement from him could have given an insight that was not now available.

As the case against Mehserle took shape investigations were also under way into the conduct of the other officers who'd responded to the incident. Following an independent inquiry by a law firm hired by BART, Marysol Domenici was dismissed on March 24, 2010; she had been on paid leave since the incident but BART ruled that she had misled the preliminary hearing about the threat level the officers faced that night, exaggerating the scale of the disturbance to justify the over-aggressive response.[xxxi] Tony Pirone was fired on April 21 after an internal inquiry upheld allegations of misconduct, including the blow to Grant's face.[xxxii] Domenici later appealed her dismissal and a further investigation found that she had not intentionally misled the hearing; the arbitrator ruled that she be reinstated with full back pay. Although she had just graduated from the firefighter's academy in Pittsburg she said she would rejoin the BART force. Pirone appealed too, but soon ran into more trouble. He started claiming unemployment benefits soon after losing his job, which was fine. He kept on claiming them after he joined the Army National Guard, started working for them full-time and deployed to Afghanistan on full active duty pay, which wasn't. On April 9 2013 he was charged with grand theft and making false statements. As he was currently serving in Afghanistan his trial was postponed and will happen in 2014.[xxxiii]

Chapter 8: The Case

The first stage in bringing Mehserle to trial was the bail hearing, which took place on January 30 at Alameda County Superior Court.[xxxiv] Mehserle had earlier been represented by Christopher Miller, but had now hired Michael Rains to lead his defense. Rains had a track record of defending police officers against abuse charges; in 2003 he'd successfully represented one of the "Oakland Riders," a group of four Oakland Police Department members who were accused of using violence and planted evidence to arrest suspected drug dealers. When Mehserle selected him he was also representing baseball star Barry Bonds in a perjury case.[xxxv] Now Rains introduced the claim that Mehserle had drawn the wrong weapon by mistake, a suggestion that had earlier been made by BART but not - at least publicly - by Mehserle himself. In fact the court knew that Mehserle had previously told fellow officers he thought Grant had a gun. Judge Jacobson was skeptical about this and believed Mehserle was now changing his story. Rains persisted, though, and told the court he had eyewitness testimony that Mehserle had said he was going to use his Taser on Grant. He also claimed that Grant and his friends had been resisting vigorously enough to rule out malice on Mehserle's part. Jacobson took a dim view of this and set bail at $3 million, saying bail at this level would "go a long way towards ensuring future appearances in court." Hearing the figure Mehserle's father Todd shook his head and whispered "Oh my God." A sum that size was far beyond the family's ability to pay, but Jacobson explained that Mehserle's apparent change of story, his unmarried status and the fact he'd gone to Nevada after the shooting combined to make him a flight risk. Mehserle managed to find a bondsman willing to take the risk, though, and on February 6 he was released on bail.[xxxvi]

The preliminary hearing, again at Alameda County Superior Court, began on May 27, 2009. Mehserle was present but didn't take the stand. Instead both prosecution and defense brought in their witnesses, using their testimony to argue their cases. The prosecution said that Mehserle's actions added up to a clear case of murder; Rains replied that his client had made a mistake and the correct charge would be involuntary manslaughter. He also introduced Domenici as a witness; she testified that Grant and his friends had been yelling obscenities at her and ignored her orders for them to sit down, and that she felt fearful because of the shouting coming from the detainees and the growing crowd. Judge Don Clay, working from Mehserle's earlier statements that he'd thought Grant had a gun, rejected the claim that he had mistaken the pistol for the Taser. He also rejected a motion by Rains to have Orloff and the Alameda County prosecutors removed from the case on the grounds that by trying to interview Mehserle after he'd hired an attorney they had prejudiced his defense.

The plea hearing was held on June 19, and Mehserle entered a plea of not guilty to murder. The jury trial was scheduled to begin in October, but Rains argued for a change of venue, claiming that there would not be an impartial jury if the trial were held in Alameda County. Judge Jacobson reviewed the media coverage of the case as well as the unrest it had provoked, and agreed; on October 16 Rains' plea was granted. Los Angeles was chosen as the new location on November 19 and LA County Judge Robert Perry was assigned the case.

On February 19, 2010 Perry held a hearing to discuss two issues. The defense had requested a reduction in Mehserle's bail and again sought the removal of Alameda County prosecutors from the case. Perry rejected both motions and set a deadline of April 23 for pretrial motions, with a further hearing to discuss them on May 7.[xxxvii] At that hearing he accepted Rains' request to discuss Grant's conviction for possessing a gun and attempting to escape arrest, which Rains had argued was important to understanding how he would have reacted when threatened with arrest again.

Jury selection took place on June 8. The candidates were racially mixed, but Rains had been applying pressure because of the perception that the shooting had a racial element. The jury pool was whittled down until it only contained three blacks, and Rains then used peremptory challenges to have them excluded. This left a jury of eight women and four men; seven whites, four Hispanics and one East Indian.[xxxviii] There were protests about this, and Grant's family voiced concerns that the makeup of the jury meant an acquittal was likely. There were also claims that six of the jurors had connections to law enforcement through family or friends, or even having jobs where they worked alongside the police. Two more candidates with stronger police links were dismissed by prosecutor David Stein.[xxxix] Not everyone found a problem though. Grant's uncle Cephus Johnson said he'd have liked to see black jurors but it didn't really matter; he was more concerned about defense attempts to exclude evidence. Journalist Tammerlin Drummond, who had earlier criticized the rioters for risking having the trial location moved, said that it was "naïve, and frankly racist" to argue that a juror would be influenced by race and pointed out that white voters had been happy to elect a black President.[xl]

Chapter 9: The Trial

The murder trial of Johannes Mehserle began on June 10, 2010 in Los Angeles Superior Court. The first day was taken up by the prosecution's presentation of the video evidence, which Rains had predictably failed to have excluded. The defense objection to the footage - a simultaneous collage of all the different videos - was that its editing was suspect, but it was undeniably a clear depiction of what had happened and it was central to the prosecution case. Stein also introduced a surprise - a photo taken by Oscar Grant with his phone shortly before he was shot. It showed Mehserle and he was aiming a weapon at Grant. It wasn't the SIG P226 though; it was his Taser. Mehserle had drawn the Taser, pointed it at Grant then reholstered it. Shortly afterwards he had drawn the pistol and fired the fatal shot. It was a blow to the defense claim of weapons confusion; not a fatal one by any means, but still a blow. Stein went on to state that the situation had been escalated by Pirone and Mehserle, not by Grant and his friends.

The Witnesses

On Friday Sofina Mesa took the stand. She hadn't spoken in public about that night before and her testimony was keenly anticipated. She didn't talk about events on the train, though, and couldn't shed any light on what had happened on the platform - she'd been downstairs when it all happened. She did testify that she'd called Grant twice, however, and cell phone records backed her up - there had been two calls between her phone and Grant's, at 2:05 and 2:09. A third call, she said, had gone unanswered. It had been made after Grant was shot. Stein said the call was evidence that Grant, who Mesa said seemed frightened, had no intention of resisting officers. Rains tried hard to discredit Mesa as a witness; she remembered only one phone call, but the records showed two.[xli] Given the stress of the situation, though, that would be an easy mistake to make. Minutes after talking to Grant she'd heard a shot, then seen him brought downstairs on a stretcher and loaded into an ambulance. It would hardly be a surprise if she was confused about a few rushed calls.

One of the most crucial witnesses was Carlos Reyes, who spoke on June 14. A friend of Grant for ten years, he'd been inches from him - actually partly under him - when the fatal shot was fired. Both defense and prosecution had high hopes that Reyes' testimony would help them. Stein seized on what Reyes said about Grant's lack of resistance while Mehserle was trying to cuff him. Rains was pleased at what the witness had to say about Mehserle's reaction after firing - he clearly heard him say "Oh shit, I shot him."

Three female passengers also testified about Grant's lack of resistance, although Pamela Caneva - who described Pirone as "very angry, very hostile and very mean" - did say Mehserle seemed to be having a lot of trouble cuffing him. "I thought, he must be strong," she said, referring to Grant. Of course if Grant was being crushed by Pirone's weight he could have been struggling without meaning to resist arrest.

The witness everyone wanted to hear from most was Mehserle himself. On June 24 he walked into the witness stand and spoke for about 90 minutes. Those in the court noticed that he seemed nervous, and much younger than his 28 years - boyish, in fact. He didn't talk about why he shot Oscar Grant. Mostly his testimony was about how little Taser training he'd received. Of the group on the platform, he said, Grant and Jackie Bryson seemed the most upset, but he said he'd talked to them and managed to calm them down.[xlii]

Closing Arguments

On Friday July 2 prosecutor Stein stood up to give his closing argument. He started by reminding the jury that police officers are expected to show the highest standards of duty and professionalism, but that when they came to believe they had the right to abuse people the inevitable result was "chaos, distrust and disorder."[xliii] He went on to restate the evidence that he believed made Grant's death second-degree murder, telling the jury that in his opinion Mehserle meant to draw his pistol all along.

When Rains gave his own closing argument he questioned why Mehserle would have deliberately murdered someone on a brightly lit platform in front of hundreds of people. It made no sense, he said. Rains spoke for an hour and his main theme, as it had been all through the trial, was that Mehserle had made a tragic mistake. He emphasized how bad his client felt about what had happened and that he was pleased Grant's daughter Tatiana was being financially compensated.

The Jury

The jury's deliberations began after the closing arguments and Stein's rebuttal, and lasted for tow and a half hours that first day. A written question was submitted by the jury asking if provocation from "someone other than the suspect" - meaning Pirone - could be used to reach a verdict of voluntary manslaughter. With no verdict reached - which surprised nobody - they reconvened after the July 4 holiday weekend. When they met again on July 6 one juror had called in sick, so the panel was suspended. On Wednesday a different juror had a medical appointment in the afternoon and another had left for a prearranged vacation; an alternate juror was brought in and the deliberations started again from scratch. Now the written question had to be considered; could Mehserle be found guilty of a "heat of passion" killing if the jury thought he had been influenced by Pirone's behavior? Stein said yes; Rains said no. The judge agreed with Stein but said that as deliberations had started over he'd formally answer the question if it was asked again.[xliv]

There were worries about the jury, though. The trial had started with six alternate jurors; only two were left. If they ran out a mistrial would be declared.

End of the Wait

On Thursday 8 July, at 2:10 p.m., the jury announced that they had reached a verdict. Over two days they had deliberated for six and a half hours and now they'd made their decision. As soon as that was announced people started packing into the court, desperate to hear the announcement scheduled for 4:00 p.m. Others were less enthusiastic. When it was announced that the verdict was due thousands of people, fearing more violence, fled from Oakland. BART trains out of town were crammed with passengers and heavy traffic flowed out on Interstates 880 and 980. Some businesses started boarding up their windows in anticipation.[xlv]

Just before 4:00 the jury filed back into the courtroom and the long-awaited verdicts were announced on each of the three charges. Second degree murder: Not guilty. Voluntary manslaughter: Not guilty. Involuntary manslaughter: *Guilty.*

The jury also found Mehserle guilty on a gun enhancement charge. This was always going to be controversial. It greatly increased the sentence he could expect to serve, adding up to a 10-year increase as well as making him ineligible for probation and increasing the minimum time inside from 50% of his sentence to 85%. On the other hand the gun enhancement law is there to deter criminals from carrying guns, by making it a risky option to go armed. Mehserle hadn't decided to carry a gun that night; it was part of his duty equipment. Almost as soon as the verdict was announced speculation began that the enhancement would be dropped at sentencing.

There was plenty more speculation too. The Grant family were worried that the verdict meant Mehserle might get away with probation, which they felt was inadequate. Wanda Johnson called tearfully to God for justice. She would have to wait, though. Sentencing was put off until August 6, later extended to November 5 to allow more motions to be heard. Although Mehserle had been free on a $3 million bond he was immediately cuffed and taken to the cells after the verdict was announced.

Reactions

Trouble had been expected if the verdict wasn't guilty of murder, and precautions had been taken - planning for the policing of disturbances had begun months ahead of the verdict and forces outside Oakland were on standby to send reinforcements if needed. Grant's family and civil rights groups called for any protests to be peaceful, with his grandfather Oscar Grant saying "Please, let's keep peace. I know what went on down there was wrong. Please don't tear up the Bay Area. Don't dishonor my grandson's death by tearing up Oakland."[xlvi] Most people listened; crowds had gathered early in the day and there were many meetings, including at five "speakout centers" set up through the area to let people vent their feelings. While these were often heated and emotional they remained peaceful, even after the verdict was announced. Feelings were mixed; while there was general discontent that Mehserle had escaped a murder verdict many saw it as a positive step that he had at least been convicted of something, as US police officers are often perceived as being almost immune from prosecution.

As community leaders had feared, though, other groups were present too. These included anarchists who were determined to cause trouble. By 5:30 p.m. a group of protesters had surrounded police on 13th and Broadway and were pelting them with missiles. They were dispersed, but later larger groups assembled round the same area. Police confined them on Broadway between 13th and 14th, but tensions continued to rise. Finally the police declared an unlawful assembly and ordered the crowd to disperse.

They didn't. Looting quickly broke out; a Footlocker store was smashed open and robbed, with the thieves scattering empty shoe boxes in the street. Next a bank was invaded and vandalized. Fighting broke out along the disputed length of Broadway as police tried to detain or drive off groups of rioters. A restaurant had its windows smashed and rocks were thrown through the glass into an art gallery; its owner's car, parked out front, was vandalized by the rioters as she watched helplessly. Anarchist graffiti - "Say no to work. Say yes to looting." - was sprayed on one building. One shop was spared from destruction; it had a sign outside saying, under a photo of Grant, "Do not destroy. Black owned." The owner was lucky that helped, because many of the most destructive rioters were white. In all 83 arrests were made, over 60 of whom didn't come from Oakland. Among those arrested were rioters carrying sawed-off baseball bats and Molotov cocktails. One masked demonstrator was picked up while filling a canister at a gas station.[xlvii]

After the verdict was announced the US Justice
Department opened a civil rights case against
Mehserle and called for assistance from the US
Attorney's office in San Francisco and the FBI.
Under the separate sovereigns exception to the
double jeopardy rule the federal government
could launch a new prosecution for the shooting.

Sentencing

On November 5 Judge Perry took the chair once more. The sentence he announced could have explosive effects, and the wide range of options available just made the decision more difficult. On one hand he could waive the gun enhancement and sentence Mehserle to probation. On the other he could give him the maximum sentence of four years for involuntary manslaughter and add the maximum ten for the enhancement to run consecutively. That would jail Mehserle for 14 years, of which he'd have to serve at least twelve.

In the end Perry tilted towards leniency, but not all the way. He overturned the gun enhancement but handed down two years for the involuntary manslaughter charge. He also gave double credit for time already served. Mehserle had been in jail for 146 days in total, giving him 292 days off his sentence. The sentence wasn't well received; it was possible that Mehserle could be out in as little as eight months. There were more protests, but they mostly stayed peaceful this time.

Release

Taken to Los Angeles County Men's Jail, Mehserle was kept isolated from other prisoners during his sentence. Current and former cops aren't too popular inside, so it's a very dangerous environment for them. Because of his notoriety, though, in Mehserle's case outside wasn't a whole lot safer. His parents had already had to move home because of death threats and one down side of the short sentence was that memories would still be fresh when he was released.

He wouldn't be inside for long. Eleven months into his sentence, on June 10, 2011, a Los Angeles judge looked at his case. Including the time between his arrest and his release on bail Mehserle had been in jail for 365 days. He'd built up 366 days of good behavior credits; he had to be released.

When the announcement was made protests were immediately planned for June 12. On that Sunday up to 200 people gathered at Fruitvale BART station at 3:00 p.m., then marched to city hall for a 5:00 p.m. rally where over 300 attended. Some businesses were closed in fear of violence and a large police presence showed up, but the event passed peacefully as Grant's family wanted. Only one arrest was made, for vandalism.[xlviii] As a protest against the release order it was seen as the last chance to get a stiffer sentence for Grant's killer, but it failed. It was bound to; the law said Mehserle had earned release.

At 12:24 a.m. on June 13, Cephus Grant received a phone call. It was from California Department of Corrections, and they told him that Mehserle had been released at 12:01 a.m. To avoid any risk from protesters outside the front of the jail he'd been released through a side door.

On May 9, 2012 Mehserle went to San Francisco's First District Court Of Appeals. He wanted to go back into police work, but couldn't with a manslaughter conviction on his record; he wanted it overturned. The court refused. Mehserle and his attorney went on to the California Supreme Court, intending to go all the way to the US Supreme Court if they had to, but the legal system had had enough; in September California's highest court rejected any more review of the verdict. Whatever happened that night at Fruitvale station, Johannes Mehserle won't be putting a police uniform back on and doing it again.

Conclusion

The facts of what happened at Fruitvale BART station are clear; Johannes Mehserle drew his service pistol and fired a single round into Oscar Grant's back. None of that was ever in doubt. It couldn't have been; thanks to the cell phone videos taken by angry passengers it's likely that no unlawful killing has ever been so well documented. What the videos can't show, though, is the thought process that led to the shot. That's what mattered at the trial and in the minds of the people of Oakland. The problem was, of course, that it's very hard to work out what someone was thinking from their actions. The only person who knows for sure what Mehserle was thinking is Mehserle himself, and for obvious reasons he couldn't be relied on to tell the truth. If he'd deliberately murdered Grant in cold blood he was hardly likely to admit it, after all. Whatever he had really intended his final story - that he'd accidentally drawn his gun instead of his Taser - was the one he'd be expected to use.

As it turned out the jury seemed to believe him, although many others didn't. If true, Mehserle wasn't acting with malice when he fired. They decided that he was acting with a criminal level of negligence, though, and that can't be argued with. Drawing any weapon is a potentially serious action, even a less lethal one like a Taser, and if Mehserle's story is true he acted without the care required. If he wanted to draw and fire his Taser he should have made sure that's what he was doing. At the trial it was shown that other officers have made the same mistake in the past, resulting in five woundings and another death. That just proves it can happen, though; it doesn't make it OK. There was no excuse for Mehserle to fire a weapon without being sure it was the one he wanted to use and, whatever his previous record, doing so would prove that he wasn't fit to be a police officer.

Has anything positive come out of the incident? Perhaps. BART have reorganized their police force and improved training, so hopefully another tragedy like this is less likely to happen. The case set a precedent in the accountability of police officers, too. Mehserle was the first California cop to face a charge of murder for an on-duty shooting. Although he wasn't found guilty of murder at least he was charged with it. That shows both the police and the public that even if you're wearing a blue uniform you can be held to account for your actions. Grant's shooting marked a new low in relations between Bay Area residents and their police, but with luck the changes it brought about will improve them in the future. If that's the case then Oscar Grant won't have died for nothing.

Bibliography

[i] San Francisco Chronicle, May 30, 2010, *Oscar Grant's character, shooter both on trial*, Demian Bulwa
http://www.sfgate.com/crime/article/Oscar-Grant-s-character-shooter-both-on-trial-3186791.php#page-2

[ii] San Francisco Chronicle, Jan 7, 2009, *BART shooting victim's family files claim*, Demian Bulwa and Henry K. Lee
http://www.sfgate.com/bayarea/article/BART-shooting-victim-s-family-files-claim-3177160.php

[iii] San Francisco Chronicle, Jan 7, 2009, *BART shooting victim's family files claim*, Demian Bulwa and Henry K. Lee
http://www.sfgate.com/bayarea/article/BART-shooting-victim-s-family-files-claim-3177160.php

[iv] Oakland Tribune, June 14, 2010, *Friend describes scene before Grant was shot, killed*, Paul T. Rosynsky
http://www.insidebayarea.com/oakland-bart-shooting/ci_15293724

[v] San Francisco Chronicle, Jan 15, 2009, *Another BART rider alleges beating by police*, Steve Rubenstein
http://www.sfgate.com/bayarea/article/Another-BART-rider-alleges-beating-by-police-3254523.php

[vi] NewsOne, June 15, 2010, *Oscar Grant's Fiancée Testifies At Murder Trial* http://newsone.com/556015/oscar-grants-fiancee-testifies-at-murder-trial/

[vii] California Beat, *Topic: Tony Pirone*
http://www.californiabeat.org/tag/tony-pirone

[viii] KGO-TV San Francisco, June 24, 2010, *Mehserle takes the stand in Grant murder trial*

http://abclocal.go.com/kgo/story?section=news/local/east_bay&id=7518678

ix California Beat, June 15, 2010, *Grant's friend tells of rough handling by police before, after Grant's shooting*, Tashina Manyak http://www.californiabeat.org/2010/06/15/grants-friend-tells-of-rough-handling-by-police-before-after-grants-shooting

x KGO-TV San Francisco, June 24, 2010, *Mehserle takes the stand in Grant murder trial* *http://abclocal.go.com/kgo/story?section=news/local/east_bay&id=7518678*

xi San Francisco Chronicle, June 15, 2010, *Mehserle blurted term of shock, witness says*, Demiuan Bulwa http://www.sfgate.com/crime/article/Mehserle-blurted-term-of-shock-witness-says-3184707.php

xii East Bay Express, June 29, 2009, *BART Cop Hurled N-Word at Oscar Grant* http://www.eastbayexpress.com/SevenDays/archives/2009/06/29/bart-cop-hurled-n-word-at-oscar-grant

xiii Oakland Tribune, June 14, 2010, *Friend describes scene before Grant was shot, killed*, Paul T. Rosynsky http://www.insidebayarea.com/oakland-bart-shooting/ci_15293724

xiv KTVU.com, March 31, 2010, *Attorneys Spar Over Whether Grant Was Resisting Arrest* http://www.ktvu.com/news/news/attorneys-spar-over-whether-grant-was-resisting-ar/nKkPx/

xv Mesa Police Association News, *What Force Science still teaches about BART case, despite court ruling* http://www.mesampa.com/news/what-force-science-still-teaches-about-bart-case-despite-court-ruling

xvi PoliceOne.com, July 12, 2010, *The BART Shooting Tragedy: Lessons to be Learned*, Greg Meyer http://www.policeone.com/legal/articles/2095072-The-BART-shooting-tragedy-Lessons-to-be-learned/

xvii www.BART.gov, June 11, 2010, *BART Board votes unanimously to purchase 130 Tasers for BART Police* http://www.bart.gov/news/articles/2011/news20110526.aspx

[xviii] San Francisco Chronicle, Feb 14, 2010, *Position of Mehserle's Taser holster may be key*, Demian Bulwa

[xix] KGO-TV San Francisco, June 24, 2010, *Mehserle takes the stand in Grant murder trial*
http://abclocal.go.com/kgo/story?section=news/local/east_bay&id=7518678

[xx] San Francisco Chronicle, Feb 14, 2010, *Position of Mehserle's Taser holster may be key*, Demian Bulwa
http://www.sfgate.com/crime/article/Position-of-Mehserle-s-Taser-holster-may-be-key-3200231.php#page-2

[xxi] KGO-TV San Francisco, June 24, 2010, *Mehserle takes the stand in Grant murder trial*
http://abclocal.go.com/kgo/story?section=news/local/east_bay&id=7518678

[xxii] San Jose Mercury, Jan 30, 2009, *BART shooting suspect's bail set at $3 million*, Paul T. Rosynsky
http://www.mercurynews.com/crime/ci_11596120

[xxiii] Oakland Tribune, June 14, 2010, *Friend describes scene before Grant was shot, killed*, Paul T. Rosynsky
http://www.insidebayarea.com/oakland-bart-shooting/ci_15293724

[xxiv] San Francisco Chronicle, Jan 5, 2009, *BART appeals for calm as footage shows shooting*, Demian Bulwa
http://www.sfgate.com/news/article/BART-appeals-for-calm-as-footage-shows-shooting-3255505.php#page-2

[xxv] East Bay, Jan 13, 2009, *Rally and Rage over BART Police Murder of Oscar Grant*
http://www.indybay.org/newsitems/2009/01/08/18559668.php

[xxvi] San Francisco Chronicle, January 9, 2009, *Oakland storekeepers tell of night of terror*, Carolyn Jones
http://www.sfgate.com/bayarea/article/Oakland-storekeepers-tell-of-night-of-terror-3255074.php

[xxvii] Oakland Tribune, February 3 2009, *Grant deserves justice, but so does Mehserle*, Tammerlin Drummond
http://www.insidebayarea.com/localnews/ci_11621672

[xxviii] San Francisco Chronicle, Jan 7, 2009, *BART shooting victim's family files claim*, Demian Bulwa and Henry K. Lee
http://www.sfgate.com/bayarea/article/BART-shooting-victim-s-family-files-claim-3177160.php

[xxix] ABC News, Jan 14, 2009, *Ex-Transit Cop Johannes Mehserle Arrested in Oakland Shooting*, Scott Michels
http://abcnews.go.com/TheLaw/story?id=6647338&page=1

[xxx] San Francisco Chronicle, Jan 15, 2009, *Behind murder charge against ex-BART officer*, Demian Bulwa
http://www.sfgate.com/bayarea/article/Behind-murder-charge-against-ex-BART-officer-3254683.php

[xxxi] San Francsco Chronicle, Mar 26, 2010, *BART fires cop who helped detain Oscar Grant*, Demian Bulwa
http://www.sfgate.com/bayarea/article/BART-fires-cop-who-helped-detain-Oscar-Grant-3269358.php

[xxxii] San Jose Mercury News, Apr 22, 2010, *BART fires second officer who stopped Grant*, Denis Cuff
http://www.mercurynews.com/breaking-news/ci_14939914?nclick_check=1

[xxxiii] San Francisco Chronicle, May 3, 2013, *Grant case cop charged with jobless fraud*, Demian Bulwa
http://www.sfgate.com/default/article/Grant-case-cop-charged-with-jobless-fraud-4487473.php

[xxxiv] San Jose Mercury News, Jan 30, 2009, *BART shooting suspect's bail set at $3 million*, Paul T. Rosynsky
http://www.mercurynews.com/crime/ci_11596120

[xxxv] San Francisco Chronicle, Jan 22, 2009, *Prominent lawyer to defend BART ex-officer*, Demian Bulwa
http://www.sfgate.com/bayarea/article/Prominent-lawyer-to-defend-BART-ex-officer-3175567.php#photo-2295647

[xxxvi] California Beat, June 13, 2011, *Ex-BART Police Officer Johannes Mehserle released from jail*
http://www.californiabeat.org/2011/06/13/breaking-ex-bart-police-officer-johannes-mehserle-released-from-jail

[xxxvii] The San Francisco Appeal, Mar 26, 2010, *BART Cop Murder Trial Moved Up* http://sfappeal.com/2010/03/bart-cop-murder-trial-moved-up/

xxxviii Contra Costa Times, June 13, 2010, *Absence of blacks on Mehserle jury no guarantee of acquittal for former BART officer*, Tammerlin Drummond
http://www.contracostatimes.com/columns/ci_15278586?nclick_check=1
xxxix California Beat, June 8, 2010, *No African-Americans seated on Mehserle trial jury*, Tashina Manyak
http://www.californiabeat.org/2010/06/08/jury-for-mehserle-trial-selected
xl Contra Costa Times, June 13, 2010, *Absence of blacks on Mehserle jury no guarantee of acquittal for former BART officer*, Tammerlin Drummond
xli San Francisco Chronicle, June 15, 2010, *Mehserle blurted term of shock, witness says*, Demiuan Bulwa
http://www.sfgate.com/crime/article/Mehserle-blurted-term-of-shock-witness-says-3184707.php
xlii KGO-TV San Francisco, June 24, 2010, *Mehserle takes the stand in Grant murder trial*
http://abclocal.go.com/kgo/story?section=news/local/east_bay&id=7518678
xliii New America Media, Jul 03, 2010, *Jury Begins Deliberations in Mehserle Murder Trial*, Thandisizwe Chimurenga
http://newamericamedia.org/2010/07/jury-starts-deliberation-in-mehserle-murder-trial.php
xliv San Francisco Chronicle, July 8, 2010, *Mehserle jury done for the day, no verdict*, Demian Bulwa
http://www.sfgate.com/crime/article/Mehserle-jury-done-for-the-day-no-verdict-3259414.php
xlv San Francisco Chronicle, July 9, 2010, *After dark, mobs form, smash windows, loot*
http://www.sfgate.com/bayarea/article/After-dark-mobs-form-smash-windows-loot-3182742.php
xlvi San Francisco Chronicle, July 9, 2010, *After dark, mobs form, smash windows, loot*
http://www.sfgate.com/bayarea/article/After-dark-mobs-form-smash-windows-loot-3182742.php
xlvii San Francisco Chronicle, July 10, 2010, *Protest plan made all*

the difference in Oakland, Chip Johnson
http://www.sfgate.com/bayarea/johnson/article/Protest-plan-made-all-the-difference-in-Oakland-3182344.php
[xlviii] California Beat, June 12, 2010, AS IT HAPPENED: *Oakland protesters rally on eve of Mehserle jail release*, Andrew Leonard
http://www.californiabeat.org/2011/06/12/live-blog-oakland-protesters-rally-on-eve-of-mehserle-jail-release